IN THE HEART OF AMERICA

Naomi Wallace

BROADWAY PLAY PUBLISHING INC
New York
www.broadwayplaypublishing.com
info@broadwayplaypublishing.com

Cover art by Bruce McLeod

First published by B P P I in December 1997 in *Plays By Naomi Wallace*
First printing, this edition: December 2018
I S B N: 978-0-88145-793-3

Book design: Marie Donovan
Page make-up: Adobe InDesign
Typeface: Palatino

IN THE HEART OF AMERICA had its first
performance on 3 August 1994 at the Bush Theater in
London. The cast and creative contributors were:

CRAVER PERRY .... Richard Dormer
REMZI SABOURA .... Zubin Varla
FAIROUZ SABOURA .... Sasha Hails
LUE MING .... Toshie Ogura
BOXLER .... Robert Glenister

Director .... Dominic Dromgoole
Design .... Angela Davis
Lighting .... Paul Russell

CHARACTERS & SETTING

CRAVER PERRY, *white*
REMZI SABOURA, *early twenties, Arab-American*
FAIROUZ SABOURA, REMZI's *sister*
LUE MING, *Vietnamese*
BOXLER, *white*

Time: The present and the past

Place: A motel room, a military camp in Saudi Arabia, another room, the Iraqi desert

Set: Minimal and not "realistic"

And I await those who return,
who come knowing my times of death.
I love you when I love you not.
The walls of Babylon are close
in the daylight, and your eyes
are big, and your face looms
large in the light.

It is as if you have not been born yet,
we have not separated, and you
have not felled me, as if above
the storm tops every speech is
beautiful, every reunion,
a farewell.

Mahmoud Darwish

ACT ONE

Scene One

(Lights up on CRAVER *doing a headstand.* FAIROUZ *is standing in the shadows, watching.)*

FAIROUZ: He sent me a horn in a box. It was a ram's horn.

CRAVER: He is a funny guy.

FAIROUZ: Do you laugh at him?

CRAVER: *(Gets to his feet)* What did you say your name was?

FAIROUZ: I don't laugh at him.

CRAVER: What's your background? He's never clear where he's from.

FAIROUZ: Can you tell me how he's doing?

CRAVER: I told you over the phone I haven't heard from him in months.

FAIROUZ: You are his best friend.

CRAVER: I'm sorry to hear that.

FAIROUZ: Where is he? *(Beat)* Mr Craver.

CRAVER: Perry. Mr Perry. Craver's my first name. C-R-A-V-E-R. How did you get my address?

FAIROUZ: Remzi wrote in a letter…

CRAVER: I hardly know him.

FAIROUZ: He wrote: "Craver and I are never separate."

CRAVER: People get lost. Call the Army.

FAIROUZ: I did.

CRAVER: *(Does another headstand)* This kid over in Saudi taught me how to do this. It's not keeping your legs in the air; it's how you breathe. See? You got to push the air up through your lungs and into your feet. Then your feet will stay up, float like balloons.

FAIROUZ: Can Remzi do that? Stand on his head like you?

CRAVER: *(Stands)* Remzi has no balance.

FAIROUZ: He wrote me that he loved you.

CRAVER: And who do you love?

FAIROUZ: I threw it out. The ram's horn.

CRAVER: We must have bought a dozen horns while we were over there, but not one of them was good enough to send her. He wrote her name on the inside of it. F-A-I-R-O-U-Z. Fairouz. That was the name he wrote.

FAIROUZ: It had a bad smell.

CRAVER: Fairouz isn't anything like you.

FAIROUZ: Horns make noise.

CRAVER: He said she was like a flower.

FAIROUZ: I don't like noise. Remzi knows that.

CRAVER: No, he said she was like milk, sweet, fresh milk.

FAIROUZ: He likes to race. Did he race with you? He's not fast but he won't believe it.

CRAVER: Fairouz would have appreciated his gift.

FAIROUZ: Do you expect me to beg you?

CRAVER: Know what we call Arabs over there?

FAIROUZ: I'm not afraid of you, Mr Perry. When I find out, I'll be back. *(She exits.)*

CRAVER: *(Calls after her)* Fairouz! *(Beat)* He was my friend.

Scene Two

(CRAVER asleep, worn out. A figure of a woman—an apparition or perhaps something more real—enters. He wakes.)

CRAVER: Are you looking for him too?

LUE MING: I might be. Who?

CRAVER: Remzi. Remzi Saboura.

LUE MING: Are you Mr Calley?

CRAVER: No. I'm not.

LUE MING: Oh my. I'm in the wrong house.

CRAVER: How did you get in?

LUE MING: I was homing in on a small jewelry store in Columbus, Georgia. Is this Georgia?

CRAVER: Kentucky. Motel 6.

LUE MING: And you're not Calley?

CRAVER: Are you Chinese?

LUE MING: Oh no. I was born in Hanoi.

CRAVER: What are you doing here?

LUE MING: I've never left my country. I'm a real homebody.

CRAVER: You speak good English.

LUE MING: Haven't tried it before, but it's going nicely, isn't it?

CRAVER: What do you want?

LUE MING: He's about five foot ten, red in the face, and likes colorful fish. He should be in his fifties by now.

CRAVER: I'm not Calley. I can't help you.

LUE MING: *(Sniffs)* A trace. Yes. You smell of him. He's your buddy. Who are you?

CRAVER: Craver Perry.

LUE MING: What do you do?

CRAVER: Not much right now. I'm...on leave.

LUE MING: Ah. An Army fellow. Where were you stationed in Vietnam?

CRAVER: Vietnam? I wasn't in Vietnam. I was in the Gulf. In Saudi. In Iraq?

LUE MING: How can they fight in Vietnam and the Gulf at the same time?

CRAVER: We're not fighting in Vietnam.

LUE MING: Of course you are. Why, just yesterday my grandfather was out in the fields trying to pull a calf out of the mud. The rains. So much rain. You flew over with your plane and bang, bang, bang, one dead cow and one dead grandfather.

CRAVER: I've never even been to Vietnam.

LUE MING: Of course you have.

CRAVER: The Vietnam war ended over fifteen years ago, lady.

LUE MING: Are you sure?

CRAVER: Positive.

LUE MING: Who won? My God, who won?

CRAVER: You did.

LUE MING: Oh I wish I could have told Grandpa that this morning. *(Beat)* So I missed the house and the year.

But not the profession. How many gooks have you killed?

CRAVER: I don't kill gooks; I kill Arabs.

LUE MING: Really? Arabs?

CRAVER: Not just any Arabs, Iraqi Arabs. Saddam Arabs. But that war is over now too.

LUE MING: Who won?

CRAVER: We had a kill ratio of a thousand to one.

LUE MING: Oh my! *(Beat)* What's it like to kill a woman?

CRAVER: I never killed anyone.

LUE MING: Such modesty! In my village alone you killed sixteen people, seven pigs, three cows, and a chicken.

CRAVER: I never killed anyone in my life. I never got that close.

LUE MING: Does it feel the same to shoot a cow in the back as it does to shoot a man in the back?

CRAVER: Get the fuck out of my room.

LUE MING: *(Caresses his face)* I can't leave now! I think we're falling in love.

Scene Three

(A year earlier in the Saudi desert. CRAVER and REMZI in positions to sprint.)

REMZI: I get more traction running on this sand.

CRAVER: Get on your marks.

REMZI: Like a streak of light I'll pass you by, Craver. Just watch.

CRAVER: Get set!

REMZI: You just watch me.

CRAVER: Go!

REMZI: Wait! Wait! Cramp. Shit.

CRAVER: Bad luck to get beat before we start.

REMZI: I'm going to visit the village where my parents were born. When I get my first leave. Want to come with me?

CRAVER: Nope.

REMZI: Don't like to be seen with Arabs. Look. I've got more money than you. You're broke and I'm Arab. That about evens it out, doesn't it?

CRAVER: The C B U-75 carries eighteen hundred bomblets, called Sad Eyes. Sad Eyes.

REMZI: What do you think it's like...

CRAVER: One type of Sad Eyes can explode before hitting the ground.

REMZI: ...to kill someone?

CRAVER: Each bomblet contains six hundred razor-sharp steel fragments.

REMZI: I wonder what I'll feel like after I do it?

CRAVER: It's nothing personal: We're not just here to get them out of Kuwait, but to protect a way of life.

CRAVER & REMZI: Flawed it may be, but damn well worth protecting!

CRAVER: Those poor bastards are so brainwashed by Saddam, they need to kill like we need oxygen.

REMZI: When I went in for the interview, the recruiter asked me was I against taking another person's life.

CRAVER: If you are, you could fuck up an entire war.

REMZI: I just went in for the interview to piss my mother and sister off. The recruiter said: "What you need, son, is all right here." He looked at me, and I looked back. Then he said something that changed my life: "The Army will give you a quiet sense of pride."

CRAVER: "A quiet sense of pride." *(Beat)* I'm not going to die.

REMZI: I am.

CRAVER: It's hot here. Why does it have to be so hot here? Can't we just turn the sun up a few degrees and roast those motherfuckers! All these weeks with our ass frying in the sun, crawling through the sand like mutts, and the drills, drills, drills. Tomorrow might be the real thing. *(Beat)* We've got eight types of guided bombs.

REMZI: I wonder if you'll see it.

CRAVER: There's the G M-130, an electro-optically or infrared two-thousand-pound powered bomb. See what?

REMZI: How I die.

CRAVER: Then there's the G B U-10 Paveway II, a two-thousand-pound laser-guided bomb based on an M K-84.

REMZI: Let's say I'm lying over there, dead as can be, and then you see it's me, from a distance. But you still have to walk over to my body to check it out. So, how would you walk?

CRAVER: We've got Harm missiles, Walleyes, Clusters, and guided anti-tanks.

REMZI: Craver. This is something important I'm talking about. Let's say I'm you and I see me lying up ahead, dead. I stop in my tracks. I'm upset. We were friends, and I've got to cross the thirty or so feet between us. *(Does a "walk" over to the imaginary dead body)* No. That feels too confident.

CRAVER: And you wouldn't feel confident because…

REMZI: Because I'd be thinking: That could just as easily be me lying there as him.

CRAVER: Right. So maybe you'd do it like this. Kind of… *(Does his "walk" up to the imaginary body)*

REMZI: That's too careful.

CRAVER: Yeah. And too scared. I mean, I might be feeling in a pretty nice way, thinking about being alive and not quite as dead as you.

REMZI: You've got a point there. You might be feeling pretty O K.

CRAVER: And fucking lucky too, `cause the blood's still rolling through my veins.

REMZI: Something like this maybe. *(Does another `walk', a sort of combination of his others)*

CRAVER: Yes! That's it! That's it! Let me try. O K. I see you up ahead of me, twenty feet, maybe thirty, and I want to get closer to you…. Why do I want to get closer if you're dead and I know it's you? I mean, there's nothing else to figure out then, is there?

REMZI: Because…I'm your friend, and you'd rather be the one to report my death than some jerk who doesn't know I exist.

CRAVER: Right. So here I go.

REMZI: Get on your mark.

CRAVER: Get set.

REMZI: Go!

CRAVER: *(Copies* REMZI'*s walk, but not quite as well)* That didn't feel right.

REMZI: Your shoulders are too tight. Loosen up. See it before you, my body up ahead.

CRAVER: How did you die?

REMZI: This Iraqi we shot dead isn't dead. He's almost dead, but he's got just enough strength to fire one more time. When I turn my back—bang! —He shoots me.

CRAVER: Where?

REMZI: In the neck.

CRAVER: Got it.

REMZI: So there I am in the sand, a bullet in my neck.

CRAVER: And it's hot. A fucking hot day, and the sun is pissing a hole through my fucking hot head.

REMZI: Exactly, and I'm dead.

CRAVER: But I'm alive.

REMZI: And glad to be that way.

CRAVER: But you were my buddy. We were friends... just friends or good friends?

REMZI: Pretty good friends.

CRAVER: Pretty good friends.

REMZI: Right. And now you have to cross the distance between us.

CRAVER: About thirty-five feet.

REMZI: And then you do it. The walk. The shortest and most important walk of your life. And you have to believe you can do it, with dignity in your stride, power, and above all, a quiet sense of pride.

CRAVER: I'm ready.

REMZI: So am I.

(CRAVER *and* REMZI *link arms and walk in unison.*)

Scene Four

(FAIROUZ *is also practicing a walk.*)

FAIROUZ: Keep your chin in the air at all times. As though your chin has a string attached to it that is pulling it up.

(LUE MING *appears and walks in unison behind her.* FAIROUZ *doesn't yet notice her.*)

FAIROUZ: No, a hook is better, a hook in your chin like a fish. Beauty lesson number seven: walking with grace.

LUE MING: It's all a matter of balance.

FAIROUZ: Not you again. I told you I don't know Calley.

LUE MING: Your friend Craver said you might know.

FAIROUZ: He's not my friend.

LUE MING: Are we still in Kentucky?

FAIROUZ: Yes.

LUE MING: American boys are so interesting! Full of secrets. All roads lead through him. My road. Your road. Dominoes in the dark.

FAIROUZ: Have you tried the other motel, across the street?

LUE MING: Calley's a soldier. A lieutenant. Of Charlie Company. A unit of the American Division's 11th Light Infantry Brigade. Very light. So light some thought he was an angel when he came home.

FAIROUZ: How do the women walk in your country?

LUE MING: Not as upright as we'd like. Hunched over a bit most of the time.

FAIROUZ: Show me.

LUE MING: *(She shows her)* The lower a body is to the ground, the less of a target.

FAIROUZ: I can't move without making noise. Clump, clump, clump. My mother always wanted me to walk with what she calls "presence". When I was in the fourth grade I had to walk home from school.

LUE MING: Show me. How you walked home from school.

FAIROUZ: It was only three blocks. *(She walks again.)*

LUE MING: Yes. I think I remember it now.

(Now they are both practicing their walks.)

FAIROUZ: There were some older children in the seventh grade. Two boys and a girl. They stopped me on the sidewalk. They wanted me to take off my shoes.

LUE MING: You should meet my mother; she has one foot.

FAIROUZ: To see the toes.

LUE MING: She stepped on a mine on her way for a piss.

FAIROUZ: Not the toes, but the hooves. They said I had hooves for toes. Devil's feet.

LUE MING: It was March 16, 1968.

FAIROUZ: Devil's feet.

LUE MING: Why, you weren't even born then, were you?

FAIROUZ: *(Chants)* Devil's feet. Devil's feet.

LUE MING: Devil's feet?

FAIROUZ: Yes. *(Chants)* Fairouz has devil's feet.

LUE MING: *(Chants)* Dirty Arab devil, you go home.

FAIROUZ: *(Chants)* Dirty Arab devil, you go home!

LUE MING: Get her shoe. Pull off her shoe.

FAIROUZ: Hold her down and pull off her shoe!

FAIROUZ & LUE MING: *(Chant)* Dirty Arab, dirty Arab, you go home!

FAIROUZ: Remzi! *(Beat)* Remzi.

LUE MING: Arab! Slope! Dink!

FAIROUZ: No. They didn't call me that: slope.

LUE MING: Thought I'd throw it in. Slope. Dink. Gook.

FAIROUZ: "Gook" I've heard of.

LUE MING: The Philippines war. It was used again for Korea, and then recycled for Vietnam. How did they get your shoe off?

FAIROUZ: I can't remember. I can figure the distance from right here, where we're standing, to the center of the earth, but I can't remember just how the shoe came off.

LUE MING: But it did come off? And when they saw you didn't have devil's feet did they let you be their friend?

FAIROUZ: A happy ending? It was for them. I think they were scared of me. Afterwards, they weren't.

LUE MING: And now you have a devil's foot?

FAIROUZ: It does look a bit like a hoof now. The bones curved wrong. Do you know what's happened to my brother?

LUE MING: I think we met each other once, but we were headed in different directions.

FAIROUZ: My God, where? Where did you see him?

LUE MING: I don't know anymore. We passed each other in a rather bad storm, and he reached out and touched my sleeve. Then he was gone.

FAIROUZ: Thank God. He's alive.

LUE MING: I didn't say that, my dear.

FAIROUZ: *(Not listening)*: He's alive!

Scene Five

(A year earlier. REMZI and FAIROUZ are talking. FAIROUZ is polishing his combat boots.)

FAIROUZ: You're becoming a stranger.

REMZI: Look. I'm sorry about the occupation and that you don't feel you have a homeland, but I do. And it's here. Not over there in some never-never land.

FAIROUZ: I hardly recognize you.

REMZI: Iraq invaded a sovereign country. That's against international law.

FAIROUZ: International law? Ha! Your own land is overrun, occupied, slowly eaten up....

REMZI: *(Mocks)* Village by village, orchard by orchard. Decades and decades of U N resolutions...

FAIROUZ: And no one's ever smacked a Desert Shield on those bastards!

REMZI: There's just no parallel.

FAIROUZ: There's always a parallel. Did mother ever tell you how she broke her hip before she came to America?

REMZI: She fell down when she was running away from the soldiers...

FAIROUZ: No. She was running toward the soldiers.

REMZI: I've heard this so many times it's a sweet little lullaby that could rock me to sleep. So mother saved father and they broke her hip with a rifle butt. Crack,

crack. Bone broke. Hobble, hobble for the rest of her life. What do you expect me to do, hobble around for the rest of my life? You're so serious. Open your mouth and laugh for a change. You used to do that, remember? Get out of the house. Throw a party. Go to the Burger King on the corner and order some fries. *(Beat)* You're an American girl. Enjoy it.

FAIROUZ: I'm an Arab woman.

REMZI: You've never even been there.

FAIROUZ: Neither have you!

REMZI: If you walked into our village today, they'd tar and feather you.

FAIROUZ: Fuck you. I'd put on a veil.

REMZI: The veil's not the problem. You haven't been a virgin since you were thirteen.

FAIROUZ: How dare you!

REMZI: I'm sorry.

FAIROUZ: I was at least fourteen!

(FAIROUZ and REMZI laugh.)

FAIROUZ: Mother still says to me "The honor of a girl is like a piece of glass. If it's broken, you can never glue it together again."

REMZI: Why don't you tell her the truth?

FAIROUZ: It's my truth. Not hers. You hardly know her, and she lives five minutes away!

REMZI: I can't talk to her.

FAIROUZ: Learn Arabic.

REMZI: No. She should learn English. She's been here over twenty years.

FAIROUZ: She speaks English. She just won't.

REMZI: You're still doing the shopping for her, aren't you?

(FAIROUZ *doesn't answer.*)

REMZI: You should move out.

FAIROUZ: In the stores, for years, she'd lift me in her arms, and whisper in my ear "chubbes".

REMZI: "Chubbes."

FAIROUZ: And I would say "bread". "Halib", and I would say "milk".

REMZI: "Halib."

FAIROUZ: She's our mother.

REMZI: You were going to be a nurse, a doctor, or something. Get your degree. Get a job. I want a quiet life. As an American citizen. That's good enough for me. Beats living in the past.

FAIROUZ: An American citizen. What is that? This government pays for the guns that force us off our land.

REMZI: *(Interrupts)* Allah, spare me! Jesus Christ! It's not my land. I'm not into redrawing maps or being trapped in the minds of crusty grandparents.

FAIROUZ: We're your family.

REMZI: Some family. More like a selection of Mesopotamian ruins.

FAIROUZ: Why don't you learn a little something about—

REMZI: About ruins?

FAIROUZ: The Intifada?

REMZI: What? They're finally letting the women out of their houses to throw stones?

FAIROUZ: We throw stones. We run unions. We go to prison. We get shot.

REMZI: Oh, martyrdom! Why don't you get out of the house and throw a few stones around here! You've got a big mouth, Fairouz, but your world is this small. I'm sick of being a hyphen: the Palestinian, the gap between Arab-American. There's room for me here. Where I have my friends.

FAIROUZ: Ah, yes. Your friends. You tell your friends I was born that way.

REMZI: You're going to blame me that no one wants to marry a girl with a gimpy foot.

FAIROUZ: My foot is deformed, but my cunt works just fine!

REMZI: You have a mouth full of dirt, sister. What is it you want from me?

FAIROUZ: What I want? *(She speaks some angry lines to him in Arabic.)*

REMZI: Gibberish, Fairouz. Save it for the relatives.

(FAIROUZ speaks another line of Arabic to him.)

REMZI: I'm not a refugee. It's always somewhere else with you, always once removed. I am not scattered.

FAIROUZ: If I could go to war with you, I'd shoot my enemies first, then I'd shoot the ones who made them my enemies.

REMZI: Enemies. Always the enemies.

FAIROUZ: There are three kinds of people. Those who kill. Those who die. And those who watch. Which one are you, Remzi? Which one are you? I know. I know which one you are, don't I?

REMZI: Go to hell. I was a kid. A child. You'll never let it go, will you?

FAIROUZ: I just don't want you to join up without knowing that sometimes I still hate you.

Scene Six

(A year earlier in the Saudi desert. REMZI *and* CRAVER *are doing jumping jacks.* BOXLER *enters.)*

BOXLER: That's enough. Take a rest.

CRAVER & REMZI: Yes, Lieutenant.

BOXLER: At ease.

CRAVER: Thank you, sir.

BOXLER: No sirs and thank-yous. We're equal when I say at ease. Where are you girls from? Haven't seen you around.

CRAVER: Echo Company A, 2, 3, sir.

REMZI: Those fatigues you have on. I don't think I've seen those kind before.

BOXLER: Special Forces.

CRAVER: I can smell the mothballs.

BOXLER: I like a sense of humor. *(To* REMZI*)* Where are you from, babe?

REMZI: The States.

BOXLER: I mean, where are your parents from?

REMZI: My father died when I was just a kid. My mother never told me where she was from.

BOXLER: Now that's not nice…. Parents owe the knowledge of their roots to their sons. A root must know its origins. You, my son, are a root living in the dark without a compass, and you have no idea what kind of tree is going to sprout forth from your skull. I'd say, American Indian, maybe. No. Could be your

Mommy is from Pakistan. Then again, could be South of the Border. It's hard to tell these days.

REMZI: Yes. It is.

BOXLER: But never mind. We're all family here, aren't we?

CRAVER: Do you know about the Sad Eyes, sir?

BOXLER: Boxler's my name. And of course I know about the Sad Eyes. I've seen them on the faces of many a soldier who comes back without his buddy at his side.

CRAVER: The weapon. Sad Eyes is a weapon.

BOXLER: That's what I love about war. The creativity of it. *(Beat)* Shall we?

CRAVER & REMZI: Ready, sir.

BOXLER: *(As he speaks he takes out a blindfold and puts it on. He gets to his knees.)* Now, let's say you have a situation. A delicate situation. You've taken an Iraqi prisoner. He has a secret, and you need to get this secret without breaking international law, the Geneva Constrictions, etc. Prisoners must be treated humanely. Please tie my hands behind my back.

(No response)

BOXLER: Do as I tell you. Use your handkerchief.

(REMZI does so.)

BOXLER: All right. Interrogate me.

(Neither CRAVER nor REMZI responds.)

BOXLER: Bang, crash! Rat-tat-tat-tat! Howl! There are bullets flying all around you. This camel jockey knows where the reserve forces are located, and, if they aren't destroyed, you and your buddies are minced meat. *(Beat)* Interrogate me!

REMZI: What's your name? I said: What's your name?
He won't talk, Craver. What do we do?

BOXLER: Be firm.

CRAVER: Tell us your name, shit bag, and we'll go easy
on you.

(*No response from* BOXLER)

CRAVER: Give him a push.

BOXLER: That's an idea. Go on.

(REMZI *pushes him, but not hard.*)

BOXLER: That's a start.

(CRAVER *does so, but harder.*)

BOXLER: You two Barbies, you think just because you
push me around a little I'm going to spill my guts?
You're nothing but piss-ants with one hand tied behind
your back.

(CRAVER *shoves him, and he falls over.*)

REMZI: One hand tied behind our backs?

(*He strikes* BOXLER. CRAVER *strikes him too.*)

BOXLER: You two dandelions aren't getting anywhere.
Hey, baby doll, yeah you, the one with the dark skin,
are you a half-breed?

REMZI: No. But you are. (*He kicks* BOXLER *in the
stomach.*) You fucking sandnigger.

BOXLER: From what I can see of your face, you're a
sandnigger yourself.

(REMZI *kicks* BOXLER *again.*)

BOXLER: What a farce: a sandnigger killing sandniggers.

(REMZI *keeps kicking until* BOXLER *lies still.*)

(*Some moments of silence*)

REMZI: Sir? Did I hurt you, sir?

(BOXLER *doesn't move.*)

CRAVER: Oh shit.

(REMZI *and* CRAVER *free* BOXLER's *wrists and eyes.*
BOXLER *springs to his feet, unharmed.*)

BOXLER: *(To* REMZI*)* That was good. For a first time.

(Suddenly he punches REMZI *in the stomach.)*

BOXLER: Pity is what you leave behind you, son, back
home, tucked under your pillow with your teddy bear
and girly magazine. Now get to your feet, you stinking
Arab.

(REMZI *starts to get up, but* BOXLER *pushes him over with
his foot.* REMZI *attacks* BOXLER, *but* BOXLER *restrains him.)*

BOXLER: That's it. That's it. Now hold on to it! Hold
on to that anger. Stoke it. Cuddle it, and, when the
right moment comes, take aim and let it fly. A soldier
without anger is a dead soldier.

CRAVER: What about me, sir?

BOXLER: What about you?

CRAVER: How do I get that anger when I need it?

BOXLER: Where are you from?

CRAVER: Town of Hazard. Kentucky. Sir.

BOXLER: Let me see your teeth? Hmmm. Trash, are
you?

CRAVER: Yes, sir.

BOXLER: Joined up because you couldn't get a job.

CRAVER: Yes, sir.

BOXLER: Father dead?

CRAVER: Yes, sir. The mines, sir.

BOXLER: Burned to a crisp in an explosion?

CRAVER: Suffocated. His lungs, sir.

BOXLER: A pity you weren't with him when he died.

CRAVER: It was like something sawing through wood. His breathing, sir. I couldn't stand to hear it. But the Company wouldn't let him retire. He kept working. For the money, sir. We had to tie him into his chair to keep him at home.

BOXLER: Shat right there in his chair, did he? And you let your mother clean up his mess. Never offered her a hand. Tsk, tsk. Went out with your friends and got drunk on Pabst Blue Ribbon. But one night you came home early, and he was still sitting there, tied to his chair. Your mother was passed out on the couch.

REMZI: Sir, this is ridicu—

BOXLER: *(Interrupts)* Yes, it is, isn't it? Because Craver then leaned over and said into his father's ear: "I'm sorry, Dad. I am so sorry." And do you know, Remzi, just what his father did to show his acceptance and respect for his prodigal son? He pissed. Right then and there. Pissed where he sat, and Craver didn't even know it until he looked down and saw he was standing in it. The piss soaked through his shoes, right into his socks.

CRAVER: When he went into the mines he was my father. When he came back out, he was something else. I couldn't love something else.

BOXLER: And you were out fucking some pretty little box in the back of his Ford pickup truck the night he drew his last, painful breath. You shot your cum the moment his heart stopped.

REMZI: *(To* CRAVER*)*: Don't listen to him, Craver.

CRAVER: That's where you're wrong. I didn't come. I never came.

BOXLER: And why not? *(Beat)* What was the problem? Are you a funny little boy, one of those ha-ha little boys?

CRAVER: What are you going to do about it? Report me? I'll break your fucking neck.

REMZI: Let's get out of here, Crave.

(CRAVER shoves REMZI away.)

BOXLER: *(To CRAVER)* My, my. I can call your father a broken-down, coal-shitting, piss-poor excuse for the American dream and you don't bat an eye, but when I detect that you're a bit on the queer side...

REMZI: Craver?

(CRAVER suddenly turns on REMZI. They push each other. CRAVER knocks REMZI down and begins to choke REMZI.)

REMZI: Craver! Fuck! Craver!

BOXLER: *(Whispers)* Faggot. Shit-fucker.

REMZI: Stop it! Get off of me.

BOXLER: Sodomite. Fairy. *(Beat)* Feel it? Feel it inside you, Mr Perry? Now grab hold of it.

(BOXLER pulls CRAVER off of REMZI.)

BOXLER: Catch it. Hold it like a bullet between your teeth. And when the right moment comes, when you've spotted your enemy, let it rip, my son. Let it rip. But remember, aim is everything and unbridled anger is of no use to you, it's like crude oil: worthless without refinement. But you've got to know where to direct it. Out there, my friend. Out there, in Indian territory, beyond the sand dunes where the camels lie in wait. Think of them as culprits in the death of your father. If the ragheads hadn't shot our buffalo, we could have swapped them for their camels, and then we wouldn't have needed the coal mines to begin with, and your father would have worked in an auto factory, and he'd still be alive today.

CRAVER: That's not how it happened. *(Beat)* Sir.

BOXLER: You can give his death any reason you want. Facts are not infallible. They are there to be interpreted in a way that's useful to you. Why, your President does it, and he is no smarter than you. President Johnson says:

REMZI: President Bush.

BOXLER: Whatever the hell his name is, he said: "Our troops…will not be asked to fight with one hand tied behind their back". As you did in Vietnam. *(Begins to laugh)* Do you know how many tons of bombs we're dropping on Vietnam? Four million six hundred thousand. It's awesome, isn't it?

REMZI: This is a different war, sir.

BOXLER: The tonnage dropped by the Allies in World War II was only three million. Now, my hands won't be tied behind my back when we go into Panama City. Operation Just Because, it will be called.

CRAVER: It was called Operation Just Cause. Just Cause.

REMZI: That was in `89. In December.

BOXLER: I'll be driving a tank there. They promised me I could drive a tank this time. The only nuisance is that crunching sound under my treads. A crunching sound, like this. *(Makes the sound)* Civilians have so little consideration.

CRAVER: You were never in Panama, sir.

REMZI: There were no civilian deaths to speak of.

BOXLER: But not to speak of, I'd say about three thousand. Now, when we went into the barrios of Grenada…

REMZI: Just where haven't you been, sir?

CRAVER: To hell. He hasn't been to hell, but he's on his way there.

BOXLER: Oh, there you're wrong. I stood outside the gates for a very long time. In rain and snow, fire and brimstone, but they wouldn't let me in. I don't know why they won't let me in.

(We hear LUE MING's *voice offstage calling)*

LUE MING: Fairouz! Fairouz!

BOXLER: Now we're ready for lesson two. How to handle women in combat.

*(*LUE MING *calls "Where are you?" in Vietnamese.)*

BOXLER: Hear it?

*(*REMZI *and* CRAVER *do not hear it.* BOXLER *begins to slink away.)*

BOXLER: Can't you hear it? Poor hound. She's still after me. Still sniffing at my tracks.

FAIROUZ: *(Offstage, calling)* Remzi! Remzi!

Scene Seven

*(*FAIROUZ *is blindfolded. She moves about the dark stage carrying small paper lanterns. Throughout the scene* LUE MING *moves about the stage, taking up different positions in relation to* FAIROUZ—*here, now there—sometimes surprising* FAIROUZ *with her voice. Just prior to* FAIROUZ *speaking,* LUE MING *begins to sing a Vietnamese lullaby.)*

FAIROUZ: I can see through it anyway.

LUE MING: This is how we must operate: able to pinpoint the enemy even though we are almost blind. Night vision. Strategy where there should be none.

FAIROUZ: Like a bat?

LUE MING: If you like. Now. Think past the obstacles, that which hides your objective. Map out the lie of the land as you remember it and have never seen it.

FAIROUZ: And forget the motel carpet?

LUE MING: Hands up! Don't you know there's a war on? Keep your head. Look for what is not there.

FAIROUZ: Imagine the land I can't see.

LUE MING: Once, an American soldier called himself my brother.

FAIROUZ: Sounds like a friendly war.

LUE MING: In the first years the soldiers gave us toffee and boiled sweets.

FAIROUZ: By the rice paddies? In Saigon?

LUE MING: Tu Cung, actually. By the coast. *(Beat)* Rush always gave me gum, Juicy Fruit gum. He called me his little sis. Once he gave me a ribbon to put in my hair. I had very long hair, beautiful, thick hair that I wore in a braid down my back. *(Beat)* But one day Rush didn't bring any gum and he took out his knife and cut off my braid.

FAIROUZ: Was it a slow knife? Serrated are slow.

LUE MING: Oh no, it was a quick knife, a Rush knife, and he strapped my hair to the back of his helmet. His friends laughed and laughed. Rush looked so very silly with his camouflage helmet on and this long, black braid hanging down his back.

FAIROUZ: It was only hair.

LUE MING: I'd be careful if I were blindfolded.

FAIROUZ: I like it. I could go anywhere in the world right now, and to do it I wouldn't have to lift a finger.

(From the shadows, we hear the sound of REMZI's footsteps.)

LUE MING: Or a foot.

FAIROUZ: I'm four hundred and thirty miles from home. This is the first time I've been outside of Atlanta. The first time I've flown in a plane.

LUE MING: I despise flying. It puts my hair in a tangle.

FAIROUZ: Could you get a message to Remzi?

LUE MING: Your brother's not accepting messages these days.

FAIROUZ: I'm sorry, but I don't have time for your lost braid. What's done is done. My brother is alive, and we must think about the living and wait for my brother to send word. *(Beat)* I'm sick of waiting. And I can't stop waiting.

LUE MING: Those who wait, burn.

Scene Eight

(FAIROUZ and REMZI, a year earlier.)

FAIROUZ: Did you get the vaccines you needed?

REMZI: Yesterday.

FAIROUZ: Then everything's in order?

REMZI: All set to leave. The big adventure awaits me. Little brother goes to war.

FAIROUZ: When we were small, the children from our school would come to our house to have a look at my funny foot. You made them pay a dime each time they had a look.

REMZI: I split the profit with you, fifty-fifty.

FAIROUZ: It was my foot.

REMZI: It was my idea.

FAIROUZ: I used to lie awake at night, for years, dreaming of ways to kill you. I thought: If I kill him, there will be no one to hate. I was investing my hatred in you. It was a long-term investment. Really, I think you owe me some thanks.

REMZI: For hating me?

FAIROUZ: Yes. Then you wouldn't be surprised by the hate of the world.

CRAVER: *(Offstage)* Remzi! Remzi!

(CRAVER, offstage and "somewhere else", calls REMZI's name, and REMZI exits. LUE MING enters.)

FAIROUZ: Listen to me. You don't have the right balance. I do. You see, I love you, but I hate you too. I have to. Tightly, tightly. As though at any moment either of us could slip off this earth. Are you listening to me?

LUE MING: *(Answering as REMZI)* Yes, I am, Fairouz. I'm listening.

FAIROUZ: Go say goodbye to Mother. She's in her room, and she won't come out. She says they'll kill you. Just like they killed Father.

LUE MING: That was an accident, and you know it. He fell onto the lily pads and into the pond and drowned.

FAIROUZ: His face was messed up. As though he'd been hit many times.

LUE MING: Water can do that to a face.

FAIROUZ: I've told Mother that, Remzi. Over and over I've told her that it's the Iraqis you're going off to fight, but she keeps saying *(Speaks in Arabic and then translates)* "They'll kill him. The Yankees will kill him." Silly old woman. She's all mixed up.

Scene Nine

(A military camp in Saudi Arabia. REMZI *is sitting alone and reciting.)*

REMZI: Tabun. Mawid. Zbib, trab ahmar, dibs.

*(*CRAVER *enters. He listens to* REMZI *awhile.)*

REMZI: Maya, zir, foron.

CRAVER: Sounds like you had a good leave.

REMZI: Zbib, trab ahmar, dibs. Raisins. Red soil. Molasses.

CRAVER: Really? How amazing...

REMZI: I went to visit my father's village. On the western side of the Hebron Mountains. Al-Dawayima. According to my mother, there were five hundred and fifty-nine houses there.

CRAVER: I didn't know you were back.

REMZI: Tall grasses, wildflowers, scrubs. That's all that's there now. Dozers have flattened the houses.

CRAVER: When did you get back?

REMZI: I went to the refugee camp nearby, but I couldn't speak the language. I could point, though.

CRAVER: We went on alert a couple of times. Lucky we didn't start without you.

REMZI: A Palestinian farmer explained to me that there are three varieties of fig suitable for preserving— asmar, ashqar, abiyad. The black fig, the blonde, and the white. Craver. I was a tourist there. An outsider.

CRAVER: You're a Palestinian.

REMZI: One old woman took me in for coffee, because I didn't know anyone and had nowhere to go. She called me "Yankee Palestina". These people lose their homes. They live in poverty, and they're the enemies of the world. *(Throws* CRAVER *a bag of figs)* I brought that for you.

CRAVER: Nice you remembered I existed. I think of the three, I'm the white fig variety. How do you say it?

REMZI: Abiyad.

CRAVER: Yeah. Abiyad. *(He tastes a fig)* These are nasty.

REMZI: You're not eating them right. You don't just plug them in your mouth like a wad of chewing tobacco. You've got to eat them with a sense of purpose. *(He eats one)* With a sense of grace.

(CRAVER picks out another one.)

CRAVER: With a quiet sense of pride?

REMZI: Exactly.

(CRAVER eats it.)

CRAVER: Nastier than the first one.

REMZI: No. Look. You're gobbling.

CRAVER: Why didn't you buy me a souvenir, like a nice little prayer rug?

REMZI: Eating is like walking. My sister taught me that. There's a balance involved. You have to eat the fig gently. As though it were made of the finest paper. *(Puts a fig in his own hand)* Look. I'll put the fig in my hand, and, without touching my hand, you pick it up. Gently.

(CRAVER starts to use his fingers, but REMZI stops his hand.)

REMZI: With your mouth. *(Beat)* Go on. See if you can do it.

(CRAVER leans down to REMZI's open hand and very carefully and very slowly lifts the fig from REMZI's hand. CRAVER holds the fig between his lips.)

REMZI: Now take it into your mouth. Slowly.

(REMZI *helps the fig inside* CRAVER's *mouth.*)

REMZI: Slowly. There... Well. How does it taste now?

CRAVER: *(After some moments of silence)*: Did you take a lot of pictures?

REMZI: On the streets of Atlanta I've been called every name you can think of: pimp, terrorist, half-nigger, mongrel, spic, wop, even Jew-bastard. And to these people in this camp it didn't matter a damn that I was some kind of a mix. Some kind of a something else, born someplace in a somewhere else than my face said. Or something like that. Do you know what I mean?

CRAVER: Haven't any idea.

REMZI: So. What's on for tomorrow?

CRAVER: Drills. Red Alert. Stop. Go. Stop. Go.

REMZI: Every day it's any day now.

CRAVER: I just want it to start.

Scene Ten

(LUE MING *and* FAIROUZ *rehearsing for* FAIROUZ's *travels.* LUE MING *is wearing* REMZI's *boots.*)

LUE MING: Your shoulders are too tight. That's what they look for. Tight shoulders, pinched faces.

FAIROUZ: My face isn't pinched.

LUE MING: If you're going to find your brother, you have to cross borders. But not with sweat on your upper lip. Try it again. Not a care in the world. Right at home. *(She assumes the posture of an immigration officer.)* Passport? Hmmm. North American?

FAIROUZ: Yes, sir.

LUE MING: Tourist?

FAIROUZ: Yes.

LUE MING: How long? How long have you been a tourist?

FAIROUZ: Most of my life, sir.

LUE MING: *(Speaks as herself)* Don't be perverse. *(Speaks as officer)* First time out of the United States?

FAIROUZ: Yes.

LUE MING: Relatives here?

FAIROUZ: Yes. I mean, no. I mean I do, but they—

LUE MING: *(Interrupts)* Just what do you mean, Miss... Saboura?

FAIROUZ: My parents were born here.

LUE MING: Here? Born here?

FAIROUZ: Yes.

LUE MING: You mean right where I'm standing? *(She lifts her feet and looks under them.)*

FAIROUZ: *(Looks at LUE MING's boots)*: Yes. *(Beat)* Where did you get these?

LUE MING: Do you think they're stuck to my shoes?

FAIROUZ: I know these boots. What?

LUE MING: Your parents. Do you think they're stuck to my shoes?

FAIROUZ: I don't understand.

LUE MING: I assure you it was an accident. One minute they're alive, and, well, the next minute they're under my shoes.

FAIROUZ: My brother is lost.

LUE MING: Lucky man.

FAIROUZ: I'm Palestin—

LUE MING: Don't say it! Don't say it! It's like a bee that flies into my ear and fornicates there.

FAIROUZ: Don't you think you're overdoing it?

LUE MING: You must be prepared for them to throw anything at you. *(Beat)* Purpose of your visit?

FAIROUZ: Your ruins.

LUE MING: Yes. Lots of ruins. I like ruins. Your voice reminds me of one. Are you sad? Are you missing someone close to your heart? Pull up your shirt. I don't have all day.

(FAIROUZ raises her shirt.)

LUE MING: Education?

FAIROUZ: Doctor. I haven't finished the degree.

LUE MING: Ah, a person who quits?

FAIROUZ: I plan to go back.

LUE MING: You can't go back to Al-Dawayima. There's no place to go back to. *(Beat)* So you're Arab?

FAIROUZ: American.

LUE MING: American?

FAIROUZ: Arab.

LUE MING: Make up your mind!

FAIROUZ: I'm a Palestinian-Arab-American. From Atlanta. Sir.

Scene Eleven

(FAIROUZ enters CRAVER's motel room.)

FAIROUZ: Did he talk to you about his visit to the Territories?

CRAVER: Not a word.

FAIROUZ: He never likes to learn anything new.

CRAVER: Ever heard of the Beehive? It's the ultimate concept in improved fragmentation. It spins at high velocity, spitting out eighty-eight hundred fléchettes.

FAIROUZ: Fléchettes?

CRAVER: Tiny darts with razor-sharp edges capable of causing deep wounds.

FAIROUZ: What is a deep wound? How deep exactly?

CRAVER: To the bone. You should leave now.

FAIROUZ: I got a letter from the army.

CRAVER: Know the D U penetrator? Cigar-shaped, armor-piercing bullets. The core of the bullet is made from radioactive nuclear waste.

FAIROUZ: They say he's missing.

CRAVER: When fired, the D U's uranium core bursts into flame. Ever had forty tons of depleted uranium dumped in your backyard?

FAIROUZ: Not in action, just missing.

CRAVER: Things get lost. People—

FAIROUZ: Get lost. But why not you? Why didn't you get lost?

CRAVER: Because I fell in love. In our bunkers at night, Remzi used to read the names out loud to us, and it calmed us down. He must have read that weapons manual a hundred times. All those ways to kill the human body. Lullabies. It was like…they were always the same and always there, and when we said them to ourselves there was nothing else like it: Fishbeds, Floggers and Fulcrums. Stingers, Frogs, Silkworms, Vulcans, Beehives, and Bouncing Bettys.

FAIROUZ: Did you love my brother?

CRAVER: I can't remember.

FAIROUZ: But you can. You will. Remember!

CRAVER: I remember…what my first…favorite was: the B-52, the Buff. B-U-F-F. The Big Ugly Fat Fellow, it can carry up to sixty thousand pounds of bombs and cruise missiles.

FAIROUZ: All right. Let's try something more simple.

CRAVER: It has survived in front-line service for three generations.

FAIROUZ: Not about numbers, but about flesh.

CRAVER: It has an engine thrust of thirteen thousand seven hundred and fifty pounds and a maximum speed of five hundred and ninety-five miles per hour. It's slow but it's bad.

FAIROUZ: If you could give his flesh a velocity?

CRAVER: The Buffs, the B-52s, won the Gulf War. Not the smarts. Not the smarts.

FAIROUZ: Or a number, what would it be?

CRAVER: Ninety-three percent of the bombs dropped were free-falls from the bellies of Fat Fellows.

FAIROUZ: If you could give his flesh a number?

CRAVER: Only seven percent were guided, and, of these half-wits, forty percent missed their targets.

FAIROUZ: A number that's short of infinity? Was that your desire for him?

CRAVER: Forty…forty-five percent of the smarts…they missed…

FAIROUZ: Something short of infinity?

CRAVER: They missed their targets.

FAIROUZ: Did you or did you not fuck him?

CRAVER: That (Beat) is a lot of missed targets.

FAIROUZ: O K: Mr White Trash likes Arab ass, yes? Is it good? Is it sweet like white ass? Do you find it exotic?

CRAVER: I'm not that kind of a soldier.

FAIROUZ: He could be a bastard, my brother. But if you fucked him and then hurt him in any way, I'll tear your heart out.

CRAVER: Remzi never said he had a sister with a limp. His sister, he said she walked like a princess.

FAIROUZ: Was he gentle with you? Sometimes when we were children he would soak my foot in a bowl of warm water, with lemon and orange rinds. He would blow on my toes to dry them. He thought if he cared for my foot, day by day, and loved it, that somehow it would get better. *(Beat)* What was it like to kiss him?

CRAVER: After the Buffs it was the G R. M K-1 Jaguar with two Rolls-Royce Adour M K-102 turbofans. A fuselage pylon and four wing pylons can carry up to ten thousand pounds of armaments...

(REMZI now "appears." FAIROUZ moves away and watches, as though watching CRAVER's memory.)

REMZI: The Jag can carry a mix of cannons, smarts, and gravity bombs. And get this: maximum speed: Mach 1.1.

CRAVER: Then there's the brain of the electronic warfare central nervous system: the E-3 Sentry, Boeing.

REMZI: If there ever was an indispensable weapon, it is the E-3 AWACS, capable of directing U N forces with tremendous accuracy. Improvements include:

CRAVER: A better Have Quick radar jamming system and an upgraded JTIDS. Able to manage hundreds of warplanes airborne at any given moment.

REMZI: At any given moment?

CRAVER: Any given moment.

REMZI: How about now?

CRAVER: We could go to jail. It's illegal in the Army.

REMZI: So are white phosphorous howitzer shells. So are fuel-air explosives.

CRAVER: We don't decide what gets dropped.

REMZI: Would you kiss me if I were dead?

CRAVER: Why would I kiss you if you were dead?

REMZI: Would you kiss me if I were alive?

CRAVER: I had a thing for the Sentry jet, but how long can love last, after the first kiss, after the second, still around after the third? I dumped the Sentry jet and went on to the Wild Weasel, F-4G. Like a loyal old firehorse, the Weasel was back in action.

REMZI: Have you ever touched the underbelly of a recon plane? Two General Electric J79-15 turbojets.

CRAVER: If you run your hand along its flank, just over the hip, to the rear end, it will go wet. Not damp but I mean wet.

REMZI: Have you ever run your face over the wing of an A-6 Intruder, or opened your mouth onto the tail of a A V-8B Harrier II? It's not steel you taste. It's not metal.

CRAVER: Ever had a Phoenix missile at the tip of your tongue? Nine hundred and eighty-five pounds of power, at launch.

(CRAVER *moves to kiss* REMZI, *but* REMZI *moves away.*)

FAIROUZ: Is that how you kissed him?

CRAVER: I kissed a girl for the first time when I was twelve. She had a mouth full of peanut butter and jelly and that's what I got. Have you ever seen an airplane take off vertically? That's what I was when I kissed Remzi, like the AV-8B Harrier II, straight up into the air, no runway, no horizontal run, but VTO, vertical takeoff.

FAIROUZ: Why don't you say it?

CRAVER: One Rolls-Royce turbojet going up, engine thrust twenty-one thousand five hundred pounds maximum speed.

FAIROUZ: Please. Just say it.

CRAVER: Forever. Remzi said to me the first time he kissed me: "What are you now, Craver Perry? A White Trash, River Boy, who kisses Arabs and likes it?" I said, "I'm a White Trash, River Boy, Arab-kissing Faggot". And the rest, as they say, is history. *(Beat)* Remzi was, as they say, history too.

FAIROUZ: Remzi is dead, isn't he?

CRAVER: I said he was history. That's something else.

FAIROUZ: How can this be funny to you?

CRAVER: If you saw your brother lying dead in the sand, just what would you say to him? Imagine it. There he is. Dead on the sand. A bullet in his neck.

FAIROUZ: Bled to death?

CRAVER: Maybe. What would you do?

(FAIROUZ touches CRAVER's face.)

CRAVER: Like that? Would you touch Remzi like that? What if he didn't have a face? What if his face were gone too?

(FAIROUZ kisses CRAVER on the cheek.)

CRAVER: That would take a lot of guts if he didn't have a face.

FAIROUZ: What was it for? You're of no use to me. Just a dead brother now. Zero. No more Remzi to hate. No more Remzi...

CRAVER: ...to love. That's right. Do you think we're doing it too, falling in love?

FAIROUZ: *(Moves away from* CRAVER*)* Would Remzi like that? *(Beat)* Do you like to watch or do you like to kill? You haven't tried dying yet, have you? Perhaps you should.

CRAVER: There's nothing wrong with your foot.

FAIROUZ: You're kind. I see why Remzi was so attached to you.

*(*REMZI *enters, unobserved by either* CRAVER *or* FAIROUZ*.)*

FAIROUZ: My brother was the kind that watched. Is he the other kind now, Mr Perry? *(Beat)* I think I'm going to scream.

*(*CRAVER *backs away, watching the two of them, as though he is seeing them both in the past.* REMZI *holds her foot.)*

REMZI: *(Talking to her gently)* Just once more.

FAIROUZ: I can't. I can't

REMZI: You've got to do it or you'll never walk right. Just once more.

FAIROUZ: Just once more. Only once more. Will it be better then?

REMZI: Soon. It will be better soon.

*(*REMZI *twists her foot, and she lets out a sound of pain that is part scream and part the low, deep sound of a horn.)*

END ACT ONE

ACT TWO

Scene One

(LUE MING *appears. She summons up the Gulf War: the sounds of jets, bombs, guns. The war sounds continue through the following invocation.*)

LUE MING: My sweet. My love. Come out from your hiding. Oh, my little angel, my tropical fish. Swim to me through the corridors of air. I am waiting for you. Come home. Come home.

(*The war sounds stop.*)

LUE MING: Yes. Yes. It's you.

(BOXLER *appears.*)

LUE MING: It is always, only you, could ever be you.

BOXLER: Boxler.

LUE MING: Is that it now, "Boxler"?

BOXLER: I have nothing to say to you.

LUE MING: You're looking so well. So robust. So alive. And happy?

BOXLER: When I'm training my girls.

LUE MING: And what do you teach them?

BOXLER: Are you enjoying your visit?

LUE MING: Some of your cities make me feel right at home. Burned out, bodies in the street, the troops restoring order. They're so much like Vietnam.

BOXLER: You're Vietcong, aren't you?

LUE MING: I hear your record sold over two hundred thousand copies. You're a pop star.

BOXLER: That was thirty…twenty-five…

LUE MING: Twenty-one years ago. Just how much time did you get?

BOXLER: I got labor for life, but three days later I was out of the stockade, courtesy of President Nick. Then I got thirty-five months in my bachelor pad at Fort Benning with my dog, my myna bird, and my tank full of tropical fish.

LUE MING: Could you sing it for me? That song?
(Sings the following to the tune of "The Battle Hymn of the Republic":)
My name is Rusty Calley
I'm a soldier of this land!

BOXLER: I'm a hero, you know. I'm a hero, and you're a dead gook.

LUE MING: Don't try to sweet-talk me. It won't work.

BOXLER: They took care of me. Friends in high places. I have a jewelry store and a Mercedes. I have a lot to be grateful for.

LUE MING: Have you missed me terribly?

BOXLER: I'm sorry, but I can't place you.

LUE MING: Take a look at my face, closely.

BOXLER: Nope.

LUE MING: You'll remember the walk. There is no one in the world who walks like Lue Ming. *(She walks.)*

BOXLER: Sorry.

LUE MING: How is it I can remember you and you can't remember me?

BOXLER: What's done is done.

LUE MING: And what's done is often done again and done again.

Scene Two

(CRAVER and REMZI are watching the bombs dropping over Baghdad from a long distance. We hear the muffled thuds of the bombs and see beautiful flashes of light far off.)

REMZI: One, two. And there. Three. Look at it. Cotton candy. Carnival. Dancing. Craver. You're missing it. That one! *(Beat)* "And all the king's horses and all the king's men…"

CRAVER: "Couldn't put Humpty together again."

(An even bigger flash of lights. CRAVER joins him. They both watch.)

REMZI: Do you think he really wanted to be whole again?

CRAVER: Who?

REMZI: The egg.

CRAVER: What?

REMZI: Do you think he wanted to be put back together?

CRAVER: How the hell should I know what an egg wants?

REMZI: I should be dead but I'm not.

(CRAVER and REMZI see an awe-inspiring explosion.)

CRAVER: *(Sings)* Happy birthday, Baghdad.

REMZI: I think he was tired of being a good egg.

CRAVER: Make a wish.

REMZI: Yeah. A birthday.

CRAVER: If you sit out in the dark, they light up all around you. Like that. Back in Hazard. Just like that. All over the sky. Fireflies. There—

REMZI: That first time.

CRAVER: And then gone. There—

REMZI: Like. It was like—

CRAVER: And then gone.

REMZI: I was a window, and you put your hand through me.

Scene Three

(BOXLER *and* LUE MING)

BOXLER: You're not bad-looking.

LUE MING: I know.

BOXLER: But I could never touch you. I mean, really touch you. I mean I know you are human, but. Well. *(Beat)* I was a child once. Hard to believe, isn't it? I had blocks and crayons, and when it snowed I'd open my mouth to catch the flakes on my tongue. I had a favorite blanket. I liked most to roll the corner of it into a little point and stick it in my ear. Then I'd fall asleep. All the sounds around me were muffled and soft.

LUE MING: My three-year-old daughter had a blanket, made from two scarves my mother sewed together.

BOXLER: I had a father I loved and a mother I loved, and then I went to school.

LUE MING: Show me what you teach the boys. Show me.

BOXLER: My teacher made us sit in a formation, with the whitest faces up front in the first row, then the second and third rows for the olive skins and half-breeds, and the fourth and fifth rows for the dark ones.

LUE MING: Remember: You have a situation. *(She puts on a blindfold.)* You've captured a Vietcong, and you need to know the whereabouts of the others. Now be polite. You're an American soldier, and that means something.

BOXLER: Did you know they made bumper stickers with my name on it?

LUE MING: You know who I am.

BOXLER: Shut your squawking, bitch. *(Calls)* Hey, you two troopers. Over here on the double.

(CRAVER and REMZI enter.)

BOXLER: Remzi, what's the best way to make a woman talk?

CRAVER: The dozers are clearing the area, sir.

BOXLER: Get on with it. What dozers?

REMZI: We're mopping up.

BOXLER: I said make her talk!

CRAVER: Can you tell us where Saddam's minefields are?

BOXLER: This is Vietnam, son.

REMZI: We're in Iraq, sir.

BOXLER: This is Panama City!

CRAVER: We have the Dragon M-47 assault missile, sir. Couldn't we use that instead?

BOXLER: Duty is face-to-face confession, son. Between two people. You and this prisoner. Well, go on. Take down your pants.

CRAVER: Sir?

BOXLER: Take down your pants. *(To* LUE MING*)* Suck him.

LUE MING: *(To* CRAVER*)*: Haven't we met before?

BOXLER: Suck him, or I'll cut your head off.

*(*CRAVER *unzips his pants.* LUE MING *begins to sing a Vietnamese lullaby.)*

BOXLER: Jesus. Can't you even give her something to suck?

CRAVER: It's the singing, sir.

BOXLER: Remzi. Go get her kid. It's in the hut.

REMZI: What hut, sir? We're in the middle of a desert.

BOXLER: Get her fucking kid and bring it here, or I'll cut his dick off.

REMZI: What kid, sir?

BOXLER: What kid? There's always a kid.

LUE MING: The child is right here. In my arms. They all look at Lue Ming.

REMZI: We're moving out. Now, sir.

CRAVER: Remzi.

REMZI: Let's go.

(They exit. Silence)

LUE MING: I so much prefer it like this. The two of us. Alone.

Scene Four

(A U S military camp somewhere in the Iraqi desert. REMZI *and* CRAVER *are stunned and worn out.)*

REMZI: Ancient Mesopotamia.

(CRAVER *begins to whistle to the tune of "Armour Hot Dogs." Then* REMZI *joins him.*)

CRAVER: *(Sings)* Hot dogs. Armour hot dogs. What kind of kids eat Armor hot dogs?

REMZI: *(Sings)* Fat kids, skinny kids, kids that climb on rocks.

CRAVER: *(Sings)* Tough kids, sissy kids, even kids with—

CRAVER & REMZI: *(Sing)* ...chicken pox! Love hot dogs. Armour hot dogs. The dogs kids love to bite.

CRAVER: I always loved that song when I was a kid.

REMZI: It made me feel included.

CRAVER: Yeah.

REMZI: Which kid were you, the fat kid?

CRAVER: The tough kid.

REMZI: Of course.

CRAVER: Some of those fuckers were still moving.

REMZI: Right here, where we're sitting, long ago they gave us the zero and the wheel.

CRAVER: Civilians.

REMZI: Irrigation and organized religion and large-scale trade.

CRAVER: But there are no civilians in Iraq.

REMZI: Laws and cities and schools. *(Beat)* That was in 2000 B C.

CRAVER: Bad fucking luck.

REMZI: The first poet known in history.

CRAVER: Those pilots took whatever bombs they could get their hands on, even the clusters and five-hundred-pounders.

REMZI: A woman called Enheduanna.

CRAVER: Imagine dropping a five-hundred-pound bomb on a Volkswagen! Every moving thing. Terminated. Thirty fucking miles of scrap metal, scrap meat. All scrapped. *(He lets out a howl that is half celebration and half terror.)* And I've never seen guys dig that fast. Forty-nine holes.

REMZI: They were going home. We shot them in the back. There are laws regarding warfare.

CRAVER: You're going to get out of the truck this time.

REMZI: I can't.

CRAVER: Yes you can, and I'll make you.

REMZI: Don't ask me to do it, Craver. I'm warning you.

CRAVER: But I have to. Get out of the truck this time and walk along the road with me. Get out of the truck this time and help me. Help me.

REMZI: No.

CRAVER: Someone has to do it.

REMZI: But not you!

CRAVER: Fuck off.

REMZI: What was it like, you son of a bitch? To carry a man's leg?

CRAVER: We were ordered to pick up—

REMZI: *(Interrupts)* To carry a man's leg when the man is no longer attached?

CRAVER: To pick up the pieces and put them in the holes. The dozers covered the pieces we found with sand.

REMZI: Is that what you think we're doing, burying them?

CRAVER: We buried them.

REMZI: We're covering them up. So no one will ever know. I saw you, Craver. I saw you.

CRAVER: It was like a limb of a tree. No. It was like the branch of a tree. That's how heavy it was. I said to myself: Craver, you're not carrying what you think you're carrying. It's just a piece of tree. For the fire. And you're out in your backyard in Hazard, Kentucky, and he's still alive, my father, and my mother still laughs, and we're having a barbecue. And I can smell the coals.

REMZI: One of the bodies I saw…it was very…burned. In one of the vans. For a minute I thought. Well. He looked like…. Maybe it was the sun on my head. I don't know. I put my finger inside his mouth. I wanted to touch him someplace where he wasn't *(Beat)* burned.

CRAVER: Touch me.

REMZI: Every fucking time it tastes different with you. No.

CRAVER: You didn't try and stop it, did you? *(Shouts)* Did you?

(Some moments of silence.)

REMZI: Why are we here *(Beat)* killing Arabs?

CRAVER: For love? Say it's for love. Don't say for oil. Don't say for freedom. Don't say for world power. I'm sick of that. I'm so fucking sick of that. It's true, isnt it? We're here for love. Say it just once. For me.

REMZI: We're here for love.

(CRAVER and REMZI kiss.)

Scene Five

(BOXLER *appears with a black box.* LUE MING *stands watching him in the shadows.* BOXLER *speaks to the audience.*)

BOXLER: Trust me. I'm the man with the box. The Amnesty box. And this time I'm in…Iraq. Is that right? *(Beat)* This box you see before you is a very special box. It's a common device we use here within the military, a receptacle in which soldiers can relieve themselves of contraband, no questions asked. Would you like to drop something in it? You can't take those bits and pieces home with you. No, no, no. I've already made the rounds with the other troops. You're not alone. *(Lifts the lid just a bit but then slams it shut)* What distinguishes this particular box is its stench. Now some soldiers are more attached to their souvenirs than others; in one instance, a severed arm was discovered on a military flight leaving the base for Chicago. One might assume that someone somewhere would be disciplined for anatomical trophy-hunting but no, not this time. Lucky, lucky. Are you listening? I'm ready for hell, but they won't have me and that's where they're wrong. *(Beat)* All that nasty shit, it took place all the time, before I even killed my first one. But they weren't interested then. And then when they were, bingo, there I was. *(Beat)* Yes, I did it. I never denied it.

(LUE MING *steps forward.*)

LUE MING: March 16, 1968. Charlie Company…

BOXLER: A unit of the America Division's 11th Light Infantry Brigade entered—

LUE MING: Attacked.

BOXLER: Attacked an undefended village on the coast of Central Vietnam and took the lives—

LUE MING: Murdered.

BOXLER: And murdered approximately five hundred old men, women, and children. The killing took place over four hours. Sexual violations…

LUE MING: Rape, sodomy.

BOXLER: Anatomical infractions.

LUE MING: Unimaginable mutilations.

BOXLER: Unimaginable. Yes. By the time I went to trial, public opinion was in my favor. T-shirts, buttons, mugs. One company wanted to put my face on a new cereal.

LUE MING: And my daughter?

BOXLER: It's over now. They say it's over.

LUE MING: The past is never over.

BOXLER: The war is over.

LUE MING: Which one?

BOXLER: Do you have anything you want to put in the box?

LUE MING: Can I take something out?

BOXLER: It's supposed to be a one-way thing.

LUE MING: Give the box to me. Give the box—

BOXLER: *(Interrupts)* I can't do that.

LUE MING: Give the box to me, or I'll hunt you across this desecrated world forever. *(Beat)* You owe me a favor.

(BOXLER hands it over to LUE MING. She opens the lid and feels about inside. She pulls out her braid.)

LUE MING: It's my braid. My braid!

BOXLER: Can we call it quits?

(LUE MING looks at BOXLER but doesn't respond.)

Scene Six

(REMZI *and* FAIROUZ *the night before he leaves for the Mideast.* FAIROUZ *is tickling him.*)

FAIROUZ: I'm going to tickle you until you pee in your pants.

REMZI: Stop it. Get off of me! Stop it!

FAIROUZ: What will the other soldiers say?

(REMZI *wrestles her off and now tickles her.*)

REMZI: You're so jealous. You can't stand me leaving.

FAIROUZ: Let's meet up in the Territories.

REMZI: You'll have to come out of the house!

FAIROUZ: We could look for the village where we might have been born. We could go exploring, find relatives, take photos and—

REMZI: *(Interrupts)* If I get a leave, I'm going to go somewhere...fun. With my buddies. *(Beat)* Hey. But I'll tell you what. I am going to send you back something very special.

FAIROUZ: Send something for Mother, too.

REMZI: Maybe I'll even fall in love over there and bring somebody home with me. They do that in wars. Come back with lovers and wives.

FAIROUZ: If you fall in love, will you let me meet him?

(Some moments of silence)

REMZI: Now you're going to be punished for your foul and lecherous tongue!

(He grabs her foot and begins to tickle it.)

FAIROUZ: Not that one, you fool! I can't feel it.

REMZI: *(Playfully)* Oops. Sorry! *(He grabs her other foot and tickles it.)*

FAIROUZ: Stop it. Stop it! Now go on or you'll miss your bus. *(She kisses him on the cheek to shut him up)* Nothing more. Just go. Go on.

(He exits.)

FAIROUZ: Get out of here!

(LUE MING appears. FAIROUZ talks to her as though she were REMZI.)

FAIROUZ: No. Wait a minute.... It doesn't matter now.... We were children then. Are you listening to me? I'm thinking of leaving too, you know. Perhaps I'll make a trip, all on my own. Yes. I might even start a clinic out there, at the edge of the world. You don't believe me? Well, you just wait. When I—

LUE MING: *(Interrupts)* Fairouz. I get leave in a few months. Don't do anything rash. Just wait 'til I get back.

FAIROUZ: Those who wait, burn. *(Knowing now that it is LUE MING)* They won't send home the body.

Scene Seven

(CRAVER and FAIROUZ are in his motel room.)

FAIROUZ: The Army won't send home the body.

CRAVER: What's it matter? It's just a body. It's not him.

(Split scene: REMZI and BOXLER elsewhere on stage. BOXLER ties REMZI's hands and blindfolds him. LUE MING stands watching.)

FAIROUZ: I want to see his body. It belongs to us.

CRAVER: It. It. Just what the fuck are you talking about? He's gone. I don't want anything to do with the it.

(FAIROUZ's foot hurts her.)

FAIROUZ: I think I twisted it again.

CRAVER: You should see a doctor. *(Beat)* Let me see.

FAIROUZ: I don't usually show men my foot unless I take my pants off first.

(CRAVER *takes a look at her foot.*)

FAIROUZ: It doesn't smell very good, does it? Remzi used to crush grass, and dandelions, sweet clover, sometimes even the wings of insects, all together in a bowl. He was quite a medic.

LUE MING: *(To* REMZI*)*: Devil's feet, devil's feet, devil's feet.

CRAVER: May I?

FAIROUZ: You want to kiss my foot?

CRAVER: Yes.

REMZI: *(Chants with a deadpan voice)* Fairouz Saboura has devil's feet.

FAIROUZ: Because you want to make it better?

LUE MING: *(Chants)* Dirty Arab devil, you go home!

FAIROUZ: Or because I told you he used to do that?

REMZI: *(Chants)* Dirty Arab devil, you go home!

LUE MING: *(Chants)* Get her shoe. Pull off her shoe.

CRAVER: Both.

REMZI: *(Chants)* Hold her down and pull off her shoe.

CRAVER: For both reasons.

FAIROUZ: All right.

(CRAVER *leans to kiss her foot.*)

REMZI: No!

(FAIROUZ *pulls her foot away from* CRAVER.*)

FAIROUZ: Don't.

(REMZI *cannot get loose. He is again "seeing" his sister being beaten.*)

REMZI: Get the fuck off her, you motherfuckers!

FAIROUZ: Remzi!

BOXLER: *(To* REMZI*)* We had an Iraqi prisoner. I stuck the knife in, just below the sternum.

CRAVER: I won't hurt you.

BOXLER: And I slit him all the way down.

REMZI: All of you! Back off!

BOXLER: I pulled his rib cage wide open...

REMZI: Leave her alone!

BOXLER: ...and stood inside his body. I said:

REMZI: Fairouz!

BOXLER: Hey, boys, now I'm really standing in Iraq.

CRAVER: I promise you, I won't hurt you.

(FAIROUZ *lets* CRAVER *kiss her foot, then she kicks him.*)

CRAVER: Bitch.

REMZI: Get away from her!

CRAVER: Fucking...Arab whore.

REMZI: Get away from her. I'm warning you!

FAIROUZ: Take a look, Craver. This isn't a B-52. This isn't a Buff. This is a hammer. I could do to your face what they did to my foot.

CRAVER: Go on then. You fucking gimp. Go on. Do it! Hit me! Hit me, you fucking cunt! Please. *(Drops to his knees)* Please. Hit me.

(*She raises the hammer as if to strike him, but instead she runs the hammer over his cheeks.*)

FAIROUZ: How do you remember him now? *(She presses the face of the hammer to his mouth and moves it sexually)* Like this?

REMZI: No!

CRAVER: *(Pushes the hammer away)* No.

(REMZI goes "unconscious". FAIROUZ and CRAVER are alone.)

CRAVER: A plague. A flood. An ice age. That's what I expected when it was over and I got back here. An earthquake. Something that would rip this country wide open. Eighty-eight thousand tons of explosives dropped. That country is like a body with every bone inside it broken.

FAIROUZ: How did he die?

CRAVER: Every single bone. We tried. Day after day, but there were too many pieces. We couldn't get them all. Do you know how many pieces make up the human body? Two, three hundred thousand. *(Beat)* Dead. Maybe half of them civilians. We bombed the sewers, the electricity, the water. They'll die in the thousands because of bad water. Just bad water.

FAIROUZ: Give me an answer.

CRAVER: They came for us. Both of us.

FAIROUZ: But you're still alive.

CRAVER: The question here isn't how many feet were between Remzi and I. It could have been thirty feet. Or twenty-five. I think it was more like twenty.

FAIROUZ: Tell me.

CRAVER: I had practiced it with him. I got it down just right. Do you want to see how I walked?

(CRAVER does his "walk" for her as she watches him.)

CRAVER: Are you watching me? *(He continues his "walk".)*

Scene Eight

(BOXLER *and* LUE MING *alone)*

BOXLER: I remember you. I think I do. Is that what you want? An apology? Why didn't you just say so? Hey. Really. I'm sincerely sorry. I've always been sorry. Besides, I wasn't completely heartless. You didn't know I shot your kid, because I shot you first.

LUE MING: You said you'd let her live if I did what you wanted. You couldn't get it up. That's why you killed us both.

BOXLER: I had a war on my mind.

LUE MING: What is it like to kill a child?

BOXLER: You're sick.

LUE MING: I have to know.

BOXLER: It's simple: A bit of…a clump of…a piece of… *(Beat)* a piece of the future is alive, and then it isn't.

LUE MING: Were you ever in love?

BOXLER: Oh, yes. Long ago. I was born a human being, you know. But one can't stay that way forever. One has to mature. *(Beat)* Maybe it was you I fell in love with. I mean, it could have happened, couldn't it?

(BOXLER *kisses* LUE MING. *She does not respond.)*

LUE MING: Why wasn't one time enough?

BOXLER: Because I wanted to kiss you again. Naturally.

LUE MING: Why did you have to shoot her twice? Three times? Just to make sure?

BOXLER: Just to make sure, I did it four times.
And shooting a child, if you must know, is rather
exceptional. It's like shooting an angel. There's
something religious about it.

LUE MING: I woke up after you and your troops were
gone. I woke up with my child in my arms. A dead
child weighs so much more than a live one. I carried
her back to the village. When I was well again, I
continued my work with the Vietcong. I was one of
their top commanders. I searched for you everywhere.
Everywhere. With more passion than one would a lost
lover. But I never found you.

BOXLER: Just how did you die?

LUE MING: I can't remember. How long have you been
dead?

BOXLER: Calley is still alive and well in Georgia, only
I've run out on him. I'm his soul. Calley's dead soul.

LUE MING: His soul?

BOXLER: Yes, his soul and I'm homeless.

LUE MING: I don't believe in souls.

BOXLER: Neither do I, but here I am. I go from war to
war. It's the only place that feels like home. I didn't kill
your daughter. Calley did. I was inside him, looking
out, but I didn't do it. I didn't pull the trigger.

LUE MING: You watched.

BOXLER: What else can a soul do but watch? We're not
magicians.

LUE MING: Are you suffering?

BOXLER: I can't suffer. I can't, and it hurts me.

LUE MING: Is it terrible?

BOXLER: It tears me apart.

LUE MING: How long will this go on?

BOXLER: World without end.

LUE MING: Delightful. More than I'd hoped. *(Beat)* But I want you to make a sound for me.

(Split scene: FAIROUZ *is watching* REMZI *and* CRAVER, *who do not "see" her watching them.)*

BOXLER: No.

LUE MING: You owe it to me.

FAIROUZ: *(Calls)* Remzi.

BOXLER: I don't know what you're talking about.

FAIROUZ & LUE MING: The sound—

FAIROUZ: …you made inside you. Not the second time.

LUE MING: Not the third or fourth. But the first time you died.

BOXLER: The first time I died.

LUE MING: Yes.

BOXLER: That would be sometime in November, 1967. There was an old man. He was wounded. He wouldn't have made it anyway. I threw him down a well.

REMZI: *(To* CRAVER*)* I couldn't say it any louder. I whispered her name. *(Whispers)* Fairouz.

CRAVER: *(Whispers)* Fairouz.

REMZI: There were five of them.

FAIROUZ: Go on.

BOXLER: I threw him down a well. An old man. I heard his head go crack against the stone wall and then splash.

REMZI: One of the boys had just come out of woodshop. He'd been making an end table for his mother for Christmas. He had a hammer.

CRAVER: You were a kid, Remzi.

BOXLER: I was a child once. Did you know that? I liked to run naked and jump up and down on the bed. I had a bath toy. A blue bath toy. I can't remember what it was.

REMZI: They got one of her shoes off. Then the sock. I stood behind the bushes and watched.

CRAVER: You looked out for yourself. That was right.

REMZI: I was afraid that if I tried to stop them they'd do the same to me.

CRAVER: Shhhhhhhhh.

BOXLER: I threw him down the well. I heard a crack. I heard a splash. I heard a crack and a splash, and I died.

CRAVER: You were just a kid.

(CRAVER *and* REMZI *kiss, and* CRAVER *removes* REMZI's *shirt.*)

FAIROUZ: You were just a child.

BOXLER: When I killed him, I died, though I didn't make a sound when I died. My body just turned and walked back into the village to finish the rest of the job.

LUE MING: But I heard it. I heard the splash. And I heard you die.

FAIROUZ: Do you want to know what it sounds like?

LUE MING: What it sounds like to go on living and the child in your arms is so heavy and she is dead and you are dead and I am dead but—

FAIROUZ: We just keep living.

BOXLER: Forever and ever.

LUE MING: It sounded like this:

(LUE MING, FAIROUZ, *and* BOXLER *all scream* "no." *Their screams are deafening and mixed with the sound of thundering jets.* REMZI *and* CRAVER *look up at the jets above them, which are awe-inspiring.)*

Scene Nine

(CRAVER *and* FAIROUZ *in his motel room.* CRAVER *is still holding* REMZI's *shirt.)*

CRAVER: That's beautiful. Sad Eyes. The C B Us were prohibited weapons, like the napalm, cluster, and fragmentation. But Sad Eyes. Who would have had the heart to try and stop a weapon named Sad Eyes? Eyes like his. Not sad, really. But confused. Or furious. Or scared.

(REMZI *appears as a vision.* CRAVER *speaks to him.)*

CRAVER: The first time we made love, we were so scared and I started to cry. It was a first time for both of us, and it hurt. You leaned over me and kissed the back of my neck and you said over and over:

REMZI: You are my white trash, and I love you.

(CRAVER *mouths the words along with* REMZI.)

CRAVER & REMZI: You are my white trash, and I love you.

CRAVER: They caught us together, out behind the barracks. They were lower ranks. Just kids. Like me. Kids who grew up with garbage in their backyards. Kids who never got the summer jobs, who didn't own C D players. They knocked us around. After a while, they took us to a room. Handed us over to an upper rank. There was a British officer and an Iraqi prisoner in there too, and they were laughing and saying: sandnigger. Indian. Gook. *(Beat)* Remzi. Well. He went wild. He jumped one of those officers. I was standing there. I couldn't move. I couldn't…. Then somebody hit me over the head, and I went out. *(Beat)* The first time

I came to, the prisoner was down and he kept waving his arms like he was swimming, doing the backstroke, and Remzi was there and I could hear his voice, but it was like trying to see through a sheet of ice. *(Beat)* My head was spinning, and it was snowing stars. In that room. In the middle of the biggest bunch of hottest nowhere in the world and it was snowing stars and Remzi in the center of it and this one officer or maybe it was two and there was a knife and the Iraqi had stopped moving—I think he was dead—and they were all over him and having a good time at it. Like kids in the snow. *(Beat)* Do you want to know how you died, Remzi?

REMZI: Friendly fire.

CRAVER: One of them had his arm around my neck, choking me, while another one held you down. I shouted for you to stay down but you wouldn't stay down. Each time he knocked you down you stood up. He hit you in the mouth so many times I couldn't tell anymore what was your nose and what was your mouth. *(Beat)* What did you call the other soldiers when you first joined up?

REMZI: Family.

CRAVER: When I woke up, I took him in my arms. The blood had stopped coming out. *(Beat)* Five foot… eleven inches. That's how tall you were. I used to run my hand up and down your body like I was reading the bones.

REMZI: I wanted to travel everyplace on your body. Even the places you'd never been. Love can make you feel so changed you think the world is changed. Up `til then, we'd survived the war.

REMZI: *(To CRAVER)* What are you?

FAIROUZ: *(To CRAVER)* What are you?

REMZI: *(Louder)* What are you, Craver?

CRAVER: *(Whispers)* What are you? What are you? *(Shouts)* What are you, Craver?

(REMZI says the following words with CRAVER, beginning with "Indian." REMZI's words are spoken just a fraction sooner than CRAVER's.)

CRAVER: I am a White Trash,

CRAVER & REMZI: Indian, Sandnigger, Brown Trash, Arab, Gook Boy, Faggot—

CRAVER: *(To FAIROUZ)* From the banks of the Kentucky river.

Scene Ten

(REMZI as a vision, as a child, making a "mix" for FAIROUZ's foot. FAIROUZ watches him, as though from a long distance. CRAVER listens from the shadows.)

FAIROUZ: He and I. We were never children. We were pieces of children. After that. But what is a piece of a child?

REMZI: Grass. Black pepper. Gold. From a gold crayon.

FAIROUZ: Sweetness doesn't last. Bitter lasts. Bile lasts. I am looking. Yes. I am looking for him.

REMZI: Pancake syrup. Lots of that.

FAIROUZ: And I don't want to find him. Not now. Not tomorrow. But I'm looking.

(CRAVER exits.)

FAIROUZ: I don't want him to come back to me as him, but as a boy wearing my face. *(Beat)* Where you ended, I began.

REMZI: Ready, Fairouz? *(Calls)* Are you ready? *(To himself)* This one's just right. Won't sting.

FAIROUZ: And the sand. I can't sleep because of it. Everywhere. Inside my pillow. Inside my sleep. I'm walking. Walking and calling for you. But the sand slides below my feet, stopping me, keeping me in place. And the wind throwing handfuls. But then in the distance. I see. Something. Dark. Moving. Moving towards me.

REMZI: Eggshells. Mint.

FAIROUZ: And it seems hours, years until I can see. What. Yes. That it's a child. Five or six. A boy. The wind has torn small pieces from your body. With each step you take towards me you are less whole. When we reach each other, you are almost transparent.

REMZI: It's too dry. *(Calls)* Bring me some water.

FAIROUZ: Almost nothing left. I know I must say your name. Now. But I can't. There's no sand in my mouth. No wind. But I can't say it.

REMZI: *(Calls)* Are you coming?

FAIROUZ: I can't. Say it. And then you're moving away from me, moving back. I open my mouth. To say it. I say: Fairouz.

REMZI: *(Calls)* Fairouz.

FAIROUZ: My own name. Not yours. And, in that moment, the sun drills brilliant through your chest. And then you are. Gone.

Scene Eleven

(CRAVER *and* FAIROUZ *in his motel room.*)

FAIROUZ: The ram's horn. Why did he send me the ram's horn?

CRAVER: He carved your name on the inside. It took him three hours to do it. His sister would have appreciated it. You should have given it to her.

FAIROUZ: I am his sister.

CRAVER: Yes. You are. *(He does a headstand)*

FAIROUZ: Why do you do that?

CRAVER: I'm training my balance.

FAIROUZ: Remzi had no balance.

(CRAVER comes out of the headstand.)

CRAVER: No?

FAIROUZ: He said balance could be a bad thing, a trick to keep you in the middle, where things add up, where you can do no harm.

CRAVER: Remzi said that?

FAIROUZ: No. But he might have. *(Beat)* I'll go where ever I need to go. I won't leave them in peace.

CRAVER: Remzi said you were the best sister any brother—

FAIROUZ: *(Interrupts)* Don't. Please. *(Beat)* It's terrible, isn't it? To be freed like this. Are you going to talk?

CRAVER: I'm going to try.

FAIROUZ: But what is it for?

CRAVER: It might keep me alive. Talking about it might keep me alive.

FAIROUZ: I mean the ram's horn. What is it for?

CRAVER: He said.

(REMZI appears and gets in position to race.)

REMZI: I want to race.

CRAVER: He said if you blow on it, it will make a noise.

REMZI: I haven't had a good race in almost…

CRAVER: You're on! *(Joins* REMZI. *Gets down in a starting position to run with him)* Motherfucker. Ready?

*(*CRAVER *is in two realities now and speaks to both* REMZI *and* FAIROUZ *with ease.)*

FAIROUZ: A noise.

REMZI: I'm going to beat you this time!

FAIROUZ: All right.

CRAVER: On your mark.

FAIROUZ: Will it be loud?

REMZI: I'm going to pass you by so fast, I'm going to, bang, disappear right in front of you!

CRAVER: *(To* FAIROUZ*)* Fucking loud. *(To* REMZI*)* Get set?

REMZI: You just watch me.

FAIROUZ: Fucking loud. I like that.

REMZI: Just watch me!

FAIROUZ: God damn, fucking loud!

CRAVER & REMZI: Go!

(As the two men move to run, the lights go black.)

END OF PLAY

SELECT BIBLIOGRAPHY

Augustin, Ebba, ed. *Palestinian Women: Identity and Experience*. London and New Jersey: Zed Books, 1993.

Bennis, Phyllis and Moushabeck, Michel, eds. *Beyond the Storm: A Gulf Crisis Reader*. New York: Olive Branch Press, 1991.

Bilton, Michael and Sim, Kevin. *Four Hours in My Lai*. New York: Viking, 1992.

Boyne, Col. Walter. *Weapons of Desert Storm*. Illinois: Signet Special, 1991.

Chomsky, Noam. *The Fateful Triangle: The United States, Israel and the Palestinians*. Boston: South End Press, 1983.

Chomsky, Noam and Herman, Edward S. *Manufacturing Consent: The Political Economy of the Mass Media*. New York: Pantheon Books, 1988.

Clark, Ramsey and Others. *War Crimes: A Report on United States War Crimes Against Iraq*. Washington, DC: Maisonneuve Press, 1992.

Cleaver, Richard and Myers, Patricia, eds. *A Certain Terror: Heterosexism, Militarism, Violence and Change*. Chicago: American Friends Service Committee, 1993.

Darwish, Mahmoud. *Music of the Human Flesh: Poems of the Palestinian Struggle*. London: Heinemann, 1980.

Edelman, Bernard. *Letters Home from Vietnam*. New York: W.W. Norton, 1985.

Giannou, Dr. Chris. *Besieged: A Doctor's Story of Life and Death in Beirut*. London: Bloomsbury, 1991.

Gittings, John, ed. *Beyond the Gulf War*. London: CIIR, 1991.

Janz, Wes and Vickie Abrahamson, eds. *War of the Words: The Gulf War Quote by Quote*. Minnesota: Bobbleheads Press, 1991.

Khalidi, Walid, ed. *All That Remains: The Palestinian Villages Occupied and Depopulated by Israel in 1948*. Washington, D.C.: Institute for Palestinian Studies, 1992.

Murphy, Jay. *For Palestine*. New York: Writers and Readers Press, 1993.

Peters, Cynthia, ed. *Collateral Damage: The "New World Order" at Home & Abroad*. Boston: South End Press, 1992.

Said, Edward W. *After the Last Sky: Palestinian Lives*. New York: Pantheon Books, 1986.

Said, Edward W. *Covering Islam: How the Media and the Experts Determine How We See the Rest of the World*. New York: Pantheon Books, 1981.

Shaheen, Jack G. *The T V Arab*. Ohio: Bowling Green State University Press, 1984.

Shilts, Randy. *Conduct Unbecoming: Gays and Lesbians in the U S Military*. New York: St. Martin's Press, 1993.

Tucker, Judith E., ed. *Arab Women: Old Boundaries, New Frontiers*. Indiana: Indiana University Press, 1993.

Young, Elise G. *Keepers of History: Women and the Israeli-Palestinian Conflict*. New York: Teachers College Press, 1992.

PUBLICATIONS

The Guardian (U K)
The Independent (U K)
Lies of Our Times
M.E.R.I.P.
The Nation
The New Statesman and Society
The New York Times
Out Now
Z Magazine

www.ingramcontent.com/pod-product-compliance
Lightning Source LLC
Chambersburg PA
CBHW052217090426
42741CB00010B/2573